For Emerson :)

Be confident! o

Have fun writing :)

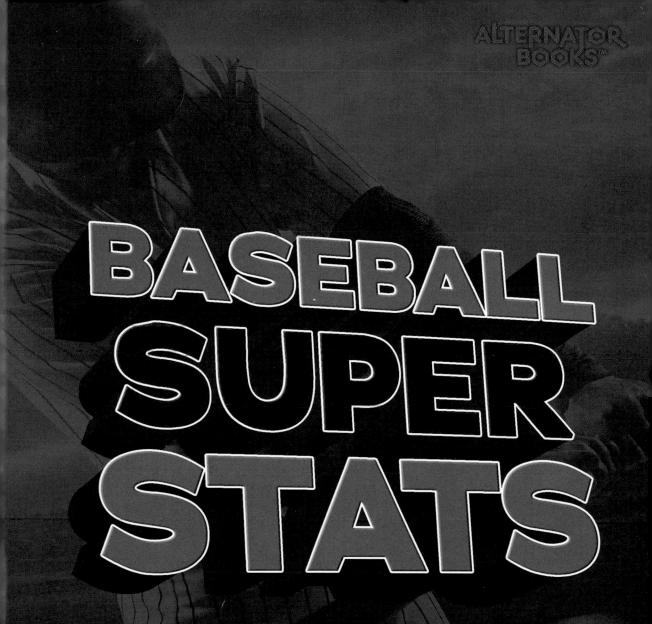

BASEBALL SUPER STATS

JEFF SAVAGE

Lerner Publications ◆ Minneapolis

Statistics are through the 2016 Major League Baseball regular season unless otherwise noted.

Copyright © 2018 by Lerner Publishing Group, Inc.

All rights reserved. International copyright secured. No part of this book may be reproduced, stored in a retrieval system, or transmitted in any form or by any means—electronic, mechanical, photocopying, recording, or otherwise—without the prior written permission of Lerner Publishing Group, Inc., except for the inclusion of brief quotations in an acknowledged review.

Lerner Publications Company
A division of Lerner Publishing Group, Inc.
241 First Avenue North
Minneapolis, MN 55401 USA

For reading levels and more information, look up this title at www.lernerbooks.com.

Main body text set in Aptifer Sans LT Pro 12/18.
Typeface provided by Linotype AG.

Library of Congress Cataloging-in-Publication Data

The Cataloging-in-Publication Data for *Baseball Super Stats* is on file at the Library of Congress.
ISBN 978-1-5124-3407-1 (lib. bdg.)
ISBN 978-1-5124-4944-0 (eb pdf)

Manufactured in the United States of America
1-42043-23913-12/2/2016

TABLE OF CONTENTS

INTRODUCTION
NUMBERS GAME   4

CHAPTER ONE
PLAYER SUPER STATS   6

CHAPTER TWO
TEAM SUPER STATS   18

CHAPTER THREE
STATS ARE HERE TO STAY   24

Stats Matchup   28

Glossary   30

Further Information   31

Index   32

Baseball is a game of numbers. The sport's stories have always been told through statistics (stats). Fans use stats to compare modern players with one another and with players from past generations. It is how the greatest (and not so great) achievements of Major League Baseball (MLB) are measured. Teams use statistics to study the game and their own performances.

What are baseball's most important and fascinating statistics? First, you should know that the sport has had three distinct eras. Conditions during each era affected baseball stats and the way fans view them.

DEAD BALL ERA

During MLB's Dead Ball Era (1900–1919), home runs were rare. For instance, the Detroit Tigers' Ty Cobb won the batting **Triple Crown** in 1909. He led the American League that year with nine home runs. All nine were **inside-the-park home runs**. Compare that to another Tigers Triple Crown winner. In 2012, Miguel Cabrera hit 44 home runs—none of the big slugger's blasts were inside-the-park homers.

TY COBB

4

LIVE BALL ERA

The Live Ball Era started in 1920 when baseballs began to be wound with a new yarn that helped them fly farther after being struck. Banning **spitballs** and other changes to the rules also led to more scoring. Babe Ruth of the New York Yankees did his part too. In 1920, he hit more home runs (54) than any *team* in the American League (AL).

STEROID ERA

The Steroid Era was a period when many MLB players used performance-enhancing drugs (PEDs), increasing power stats such as home runs. It's hard to say when the Steroid Era began, but its peak may have been 1998. That season, St. Louis Cardinals slugger Mark McGwire's 70 homers were two more than the entire Cardinals team hit in 1991. The league had banned PEDs in 1991 but didn't test all players for them until 2003.

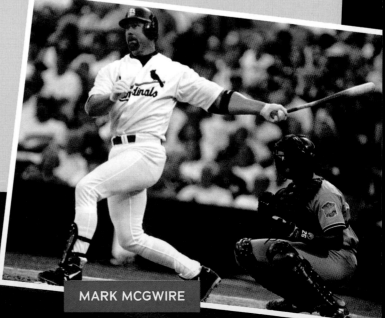

MARK MCGWIRE

CHAPTER ONE

PLAYER SUPER STATS

CAL RIPKEN JR.

NO SICK DAYS

MLB players gather stats during long and grueling seasons. With 162 games on the schedule, teams may go weeks without a day off. Every single game for more than 16 seasons, Cal Ripken Jr. was in the lineup for the Baltimore Orioles. The night Ripken broke Lou Gehrig's record for games played in a row, fans and players gave Ripken a standing ovation that lasted 22 minutes.

Most MLB Games Played in a Row

PLAYER	FIRST GAME OF STREAK	LAST GAME OF STREAK	TOTAL GAMES
Cal Ripken Jr.	May 30, 1982	September 19, 1998	2,632
Lou Gehrig	June 1, 1925	April 30, 1939	2,130
Everett Scott	June 20, 1916	May 5, 1925	1,307
Steve Garvey	September 3, 1975	July 29, 1983	1,207
Miguel Tejada	June 1, 2000	June 21, 2007	1,152
Billy Williams	September 22, 1963	September 2, 1970	1,117
Joe Sewell	September 13, 1922	April 30, 1930	1,103
Stan Musial	April 15, 1952	August 23, 1957	895
Eddie Yost	April 30, 1949	May 11, 1955	829

JOSE ALTUVE

SWING, BATTER, SWING!

The most popular player stat with fans might be batting average. It measures how often a batter gets a base hit. And what could be more important to a hitter than getting hits? Batting .300 (averaging three hits every 10 at bats) over a full season is a solid average. Hitting .400 or better has been done dozens of times in MLB history, but not since 1941 when Ted Williams batted .406 for the Boston Red Sox.

STATS FACT

Houston Astros second baseman Jose Altuve won the AL batting crown in 2014 with a .341 average. At 5 feet 6 (168 centimeters), he was the shortest player to win a batting crown since Wee Willie Keeler in 1898. Altuve won it again in 2016.

Highest Full-Season Batting Averages since 1941

YEAR	PLAYER	TEAM	BATTING AVERAGE
1994	Tony Gwynn	San Diego Padres	.394
1980	George Brett	Kansas City Royals	.390
1977	Rod Carew	Minnesota Twins	.388
1957	Ted Williams	Boston Red Sox	.388
1999	Larry Walker	Colorado Rockies	.379
1948	Stan Musial	St. Louis Cardinals	.376
2004	Ichiro Suzuki	Seattle Mariners	.372
2000	Nomar Garciaparra	Boston Red Sox	.372
2000	Todd Helton	Colorado Rockies	.372
1997	Tony Gwynn	San Diego Padres	.372

CHASING JOE DIMAGGIO

Ted Williams was the last player to hit at least .400 for a season. But he was *not* named AL Most Valuable Player (MVP) in 1941. The award went to Joe DiMaggio. Why? The New York Yankees outfielder got a hit in 56 straight games that season. Such a streak shows incredible skill and mastery of the sport. This record still stands. In fact, no one has come close to matching DiMaggio's incredible streak.

Longest Single-Season Hitting Streaks since 1941

Player • Year of the hitting streak • Team

Pete Rose • 1978 • Cincinnati Reds

Paul Molitor • 1987 • Milwaukee Brewers

Tommy Holmes • 1945 • Boston Braves

Luis Castillo • 2002 • Florida Marlins

Chase Utley • 2006 • Philadelphia Phillies

Dom DiMaggio • 1949 • Boston Red Sox

Benito Santiago • 1987 • San Diego Padres

Dan Uggla • 2011 • Atlanta Braves

Vladimir Guerrero • 1999 • Montreal Expos

Ken Landreaux • 1980 • Minnesota Twins

Rico Carty • 1970 • Atlanta Braves

Willie Davis • 1969 • Los Angeles Dodgers

31 32 33 34 35 36 37 38 39 40 41 42 43 44

Games in a row with a hit

STATS FACT

Ichiro Suzuki played pro baseball in Japan for nine years before joining the Seattle Mariners in 2001. Beginning that year, Ichiro topped the 200 hit mark 10 seasons in a row!

THE HIT KING

Of all the great MLB hitters since 1941, Pete Rose came closest to breaking Joe DiMaggio's 56-game hitting streak. Rose claims a famous MLB number of his own: 4,256. That's the most career base hits of all time. It took a *long* time to get there. Rose played 24 seasons, mostly for the Cincinnati Reds. His 3,562 career games played are the most in baseball history.

ICHIRO SUZUKI

All-Time Hits Leaders

PLAYER	TEAM*	HITS
Pete Rose	Cincinnati Reds	4,256
Ty Cobb	Detroit Tigers	4,189
Hank Aaron	Milwaukee Braves	3,771
Stan Musial	St. Louis Cardinals	3,630
Tris Speaker	Cleveland Indians	3,514
Derek Jeter	New York Yankees	3,465
Cap Anson	Chicago White Stockings	3,435
Honus Wagner	Pittsburgh Pirates	3,420
Carl Yastrzemski	Boston Red Sox	3,419
Paul Molitor	Milwaukee Brewers	3,319

*The player spent most of his career with this team.

BARRY BONDS

BACK, BACK, BACK . . . GONE!

In 1927 Babe Ruth swatted 60 homers, the most ever in a season at the time. That magical number stood for 34 years. New York Yankees outfielder Roger Maris topped Ruth's record in 1961. Some fans cheered, while others booed. Maris's new record of 61 home runs lasted 37 years. Then, during a four-year stretch in the heart of the Steroid Era, Maris's mark was topped *six times*.

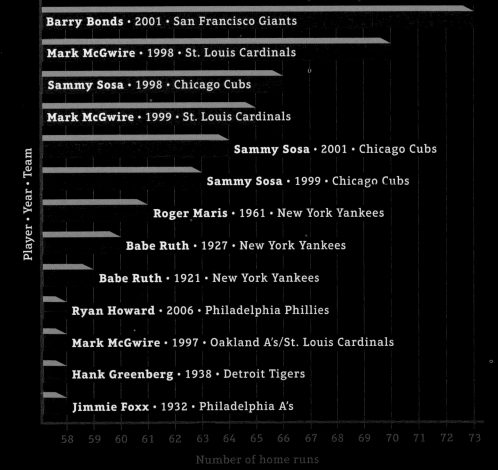

Most Home Runs by a Player in a Season

Player • Year • Team

Barry Bonds • 2001 • San Francisco Giants
Mark McGwire • 1998 • St. Louis Cardinals
Sammy Sosa • 1998 • Chicago Cubs
Mark McGwire • 1999 • St. Louis Cardinals
Sammy Sosa • 2001 • Chicago Cubs
Sammy Sosa • 1999 • Chicago Cubs
Roger Maris • 1961 • New York Yankees
Babe Ruth • 1927 • New York Yankees
Babe Ruth • 1921 • New York Yankees
Ryan Howard • 2006 • Philadelphia Phillies
Mark McGwire • 1997 • Oakland A's/St. Louis Cardinals
Hank Greenberg • 1938 • Detroit Tigers
Jimmie Foxx • 1932 • Philadelphia A's

58 59 60 61 62 63 64 65 66 67 68 69 70 71 72 73

Number of home runs

RICKEY HENDERSON *(LEFT)*

STEALING VICTORY

The all-time runaway leader in **stolen bases** is Rickey Henderson, who played 25 seasons for nine teams. He stole 130 bases in 1982, the most since 1900. And his career number of stolen bases—1,406—is huge. No one else on the all-time list even has a four-digit number next to his name.

Most Stolen Bases in a Career since 1900

PLAYER	TEAM*	STOLEN BASES
Rickey Henderson	Oakland A's	1,406
Lou Brock	St. Louis Cardinals	938
Ty Cobb	Detroit Tigers	897
Tim Raines	Montreal Expos	808
Vince Coleman	St. Louis Cardinals	752

*The player spent most of his career with this team.

Most Stolen Bases in a Season since 1900

YEAR	PLAYER	TEAM*	STOLEN BASES
1982	Rickey Henderson	Oakland A's	130
1974	Lou Brock	St. Louis Cardinals	118
1985	Vince Coleman	St. Louis Cardinals	110
1987	Vince Coleman	St. Louis Cardinals	109
1983	Rickey Henderson	Oakland A's	108

*The player spent most of his career with this team.

THAT'S WHY THEY CALL IT THE CY YOUNG AWARD

At least one MLB record will probably last forever. Pitcher Cy Young won 511 games when he played in the late 1800s and into the 1900s. In the modern game, teams have more pitchers and there are fewer chances for one pitcher to get wins. So 20 or more wins in a season is rare. Cy Young reached at least 30 wins five times. To break Young's record of 511 wins, a pitcher would need to win 20 games each year for more than 25 seasons.

HISTORY HIGHLIGHT

Nolan Ryan threw 100-mile-per-hour (161-kilometer) fastballs past hitters during parts of four decades. He threw seven **no-hitters**, three more than any other pitcher. He also threw 12 one-hitters and 18 two-hitters.

Pitchers Who Have Won 20 or More Games in Recent Seasons

2016

PLAYER	TEAM	WINS
Rick Porcello	Boston Red Sox	22
J. A. Happ	Toronto Blue Jays	20
Max Scherzer	Washington Nationals	20

2015

PLAYER	TEAM	WINS
Jake Arrieta	Chicago Cubs	22
Dallas Keuchel	Houston Astros	20

2014

PLAYER	TEAM	WINS
Clayton Kershaw	Los Angeles Dodgers	21
Johnny Cueto	Cincinnati Reds	20
Adam Wainwright	St. Louis Cardinals	20

2013

PLAYER	TEAM	WINS
Max Scherzer	Detroit Tigers	21

EVERYONE MAKES MISTAKES

What if a team scored a bunch of runs because outfielders dropped easy fly balls and infielders made bad throws? Would that be the pitcher's fault? **Earned run average (ERA)** shows how many runs a pitcher allowed that weren't the result of an **error**. The statistic is one of the best ways to tell how a pitcher really performed.

CLAYTON KERSHAW

Starting Pitchers with the Best ERAs in a Season since 2000

National League

YEAR	PITCHER	TEAM	ERA
2015	Zack Greinke	Los Angeles Dodgers	1.66
2014	Clayton Kershaw	Los Angeles Dodgers	1.77
2013	Clayton Kershaw	Los Angeles Dodgers	1.83
2005	Roger Clemens	Houston Astros	1.87
2016	Kyle Hendricks	Chicago Cubs	2.13

American League

YEAR	PITCHER	TEAM	ERA
2000	Pedro Martinez	Boston Red Sox	1.74
2014	Felix Hernandez	Seattle Mariners	2.14
2009	Zack Greinke	Kansas City Royals	2.16
2003	Pedro Martinez	Boston Red Sox	2.22
2002	Pedro Martinez	Boston Red Sox	2.26

MORE WHIP, PLEASE

Pitchers aren't judged solely by how many runs they allow. WHIP stands for walks and hits per inning pitched. If a pitcher gives up a hit and a walk in an inning, the WHIP is 2.00. A WHIP of 1.32 for a season is average. In 2000 Pedro Martinez's WHIP of 0.74 for the Red Sox broke an MLB record that had lasted *87 years.*

PEDRO MARTINEZ

Starting Pitchers with the Best WHIP in a Season since 2000

YEAR	PITCHER	TEAM	WHIP
2000	Pedro Martinez	Boston Red Sox	0.74
2015	Zack Greinke	Los Angeles Dodgers	0.84
2015	Jake Arrieta	Chicago Cubs	0.86
2014	Clayton Kershaw	Los Angeles Dodgers	0.86
2015	Clayton Kershaw	Los Angeles Dodgers	0.88
2004	Randy Johnson	Seattle Mariners	0.90
2015	Max Scherzer	Washington Nationals	0.92
2014	Felix Hernandez	Seattle Mariners	0.92
2013	Clayton Kershaw	Los Angeles Dodgers	0.92
2011	Justin Verlander	Detroit Tigers	0.92
2004	Johan Santana	Minnesota Twins	0.92

YOU'RE OUT!

A strikeout is the ultimate show of power for a pitcher. Nolan Ryan struck out 5,714 batters in his 27-year MLB career. That's nearly 1,000 more than anyone else. As great as Ryan was, he never struck out every batter in a game. No one has. A team has 27 outs in a nine-inning game. Ryan struck out as many as 19 batters in a game. Four pitchers have topped that!

MAX SCHERZER

Most Strikeouts in Nine Innings

YEAR	PITCHER	TEAM	STRIKEOUTS
2016	Max Scherzer	Washington Nationals	20
2001	Randy Johnson	Seattle Mariners	20
1998	Kerry Wood	Chicago Cubs	20
1996	Roger Clemens	Boston Red Sox	20
1986	Roger Clemens	Boston Red Sox	20

HELP!

It used to be common for starting pitchers to go the distance and pitch a complete game. Not anymore. In modern times, relief pitchers often enter a close game and record a **save**. Saves did not become an official MLB stat until 1969. Of the 27 relief pitchers in MLB history with 300 or more saves, all of them pitched in the 1980s or later.

STATS FACT

Relief ace Aroldis Chapman often throws the ball faster than 100 miles (161 km) per hour. One Chapman fastball in 2016 was clocked at 105.1 miles (169 km) per hour. That tied his own record for the fastest pitch ever!

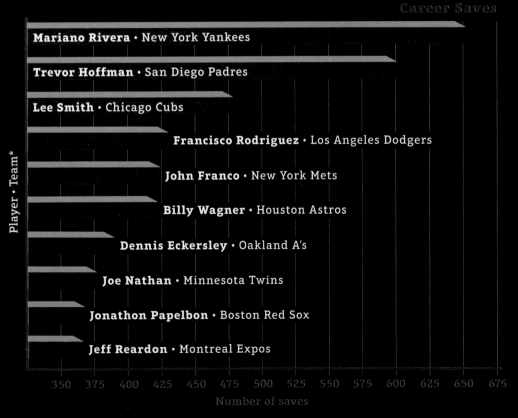

Career Saves

Mariano Rivera · New York Yankees

Trevor Hoffman · San Diego Padres

Lee Smith · Chicago Cubs

Francisco Rodriguez · Los Angeles Dodgers

John Franco · New York Mets

Billy Wagner · Houston Astros

Dennis Eckersley · Oakland A's

Joe Nathan · Minnesota Twins

Jonathon Papelbon · Boston Red Sox

Jeff Reardon · Montreal Expos

Player · Team*

350   375   400   425   450   475   500   525   550   575   600   625   650   675

Number of saves

*The player spent most of his career with this team

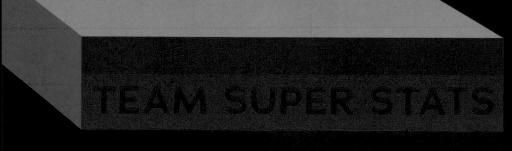

2013 BOSTON RED SOX

JUST WIN, BABY

In Little League, baseball is about having fun, making friends, and learning to play as a team. Little League teams also play to win. But at the MLB level, it's *all* about winning. Winning percentage can tell you how many games a team will win if they keep up the same pace all season. A team that wins six out of 10 games has a winning percentage of .600. That equals about 98 wins in a full season. Some years that would be enough for the best record in baseball.

Best Season-Long Winning Percentages since 2011

YEAR	TEAM	WINNING PERCENTAGE (RECORD)
2016	Chicago Cubs	.640 (103–58)
2015	St. Louis Cardinals	.617 (100–62)
2014	Los Angeles Angels	.605 (98–64)
2013	Boston Red Sox	.599 (97–65)
2013	St. Louis Cardinals	.599 (97–65)
2012	Washington Nationals	.605 (98–64)
2011	Philadelphia Phillies	.630 (102–60)

EYE ON THE PRIZE

Winning the most games in the regular season does not guarantee success in the playoffs. The 2001 Seattle Mariners had the best winning percentage this century (.716) but failed to reach the World Series. To judge a baseball team's history, the most important statistic is World Series championships.

STATS FACT

The Miami Marlins have won two World Series crowns (1997, 2003) but have never won their own division.

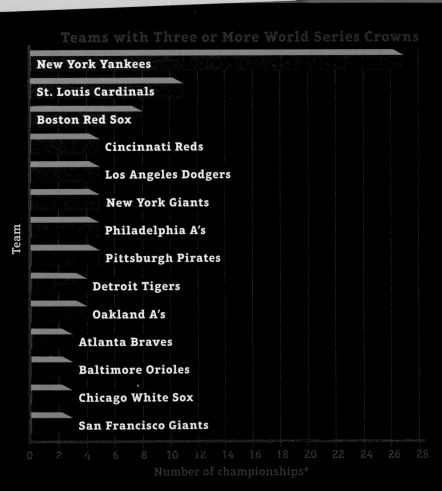

Teams with Three or More World Series Crowns

New York Yankees
St. Louis Cardinals
Boston Red Sox
Cincinnati Reds
Los Angeles Dodgers
New York Giants
Philadelphia A's
Pittsburgh Pirates
Detroit Tigers
Oakland A's
Atlanta Braves
Baltimore Orioles
Chicago White Sox
San Francisco Giants

Team

0 2 4 6 8 10 12 14 16 18 20 22 24 26 28

Number of championships*

*Includes championships won when teams were based in other cities

KEEP IT GOING

Sometimes MLB teams catch fire! Long winning streaks can help teams catch up in the standings. Or a streak can help a team bury the competition. In the playoffs, a winning streak may propel a team all the way to World Series glory.

Longest Regular-Season Winning Streaks in MLB History

Games won in a row

26
24
22
20
18
16
14
12
10
8
6
4
2
0

New York Giants · 1916
Chicago Cubs · 1935
Chicago White Stockings · 1880
Oakland A's · 2002
New York Yankees · 1947
Chicago White Sox · 1906
Boston Beaneaters · 1891
Kansas City Royals · 1977
Pittsburgh Pirates · 1909
Philadelphia Quakers · 1887

Team · Year

BEST COMEBACKS IN THE STANDINGS IN MLB HISTORY

Think your favorite team won't make the playoffs? Don't give up yet! Your team may be just a winning streak away from an incredible comeback in the standings.

1951 The New York Giants were 13 games out of first place in the standings. Then they won 39 of their next 47 games to claim the top spot.

1964 The St. Louis Cardinals were in fourth place in the NL with about a month to play in the season. St. Louis got hot and took over first place on the last day of the season.

1969 On August 13, the New York Mets lagged behind the Chicago Cubs by nine and a half games. The Miracle Mets, as fans called them, wound up beating the Cubs by eight games.

1978 The New York Yankees were 14 games behind the Boston Red Sox in July. The Yanks caught the Sox in the standings on the final day of the season. The next day, New York beat Boston in a one-game tiebreaker.

1995 The Seattle Mariners had a losing record at the beginning of August and were seven and a half games out of first place at the beginning of September. They roared back to win their division.

2011 The Tampa Bay Rays were nine games behind the Red Sox in September. The Rays passed the Sox on the final day of the season by beating them in extra innings to claim a playoff spot.

2011 TAMPA BAY RAYS

TONS OF HOME RUNS

When baseball began in the 1800s, there weren't many rules to keep games fair. Spitballs, balls that were scuffed up and dirty, and other tactics made batting a chore. With more rules and better equipment, the Dead Ball Era died in 1919. Since then the rules and the way baseballs are made haven't changed much. But for a time, the Steroid Era inflated power statistics— especially home runs.

LANCE BERKMAN OF THE 2000 HOUSTON ASTROS

Fewest Team Home Runs in a Season

LEAGUE	YEAR	TEAM	HOME RUNS
AL	1908	Chicago White Sox	3
NL	1917	Pittsburgh Pirates	9

Most Team Home Runs in a Season

LEAGUE	YEAR	TEAM	HOME RUNS
AL	1997	Seattle Mariners	264
NL	2000	Houston Astros	249

HALL OF FAME

It is a great honor to be voted into the National Baseball Hall of Fame. Only 217 former major-league players have made it. In 2016, 32 names were on the ballot. The Baseball Writers' Association of America voted for only two players to enter the Hall—Ken Griffey Jr. and Mike Piazza.

HISTORY HIGHLIGHT

Babe Ruth started playing pro baseball more than a century ago. He still holds all-time records for career **slugging percentage** (.690) and **on-base plus slugging (OPS)** (1.164). Before becoming a great hitter with the New York Yankees, Ruth was an excellent pitcher for the Boston Red Sox. In 1916 he recorded 170 strikeouts without allowing a home run. A year later, he won 24 games and led the AL in complete games (35).

Hall of Fame Players by Team

THE BOX SCORE

Baseball has changed a lot since it was invented in 1839. But how fans read stats is just about the same as it's always been. Since sportswriter Henry Chadwick created the box score in 1859, it has been the ultimate place for baseball stats.

If a picture is worth 1,000 words, how much is a box score worth? A box score contains everything a fan wants to know about a baseball game. You could write a full-length story by studying this table full of numbers. But first, you need to know what all the words and numbers mean. Use the key to read the box score on the next page.

HENRY CHADWICK

Batting Key

AB = at bats

AVG = season batting average

BB = bases on balls (walks)

H = hits

LOB = runners left on base after the batter makes an out

R = runs scored

RBI = runs batted in

SO = strikeouts

Pitching Key

BB = bases on balls (walks) allowed

ER = earned runs allowed

ERA = season earned run average

H = hits allowed

HR = home runs allowed

IP = innings pitched

L = loss

R = total runs allowed

SO = strikeouts

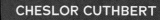

CHESLOR CUTHBERT

Kansas City Royals Batters

	AB	R	H	RBI	BB	SO	LOB	AVG
Dyson	1	0	0	1	2	0	1	.251
Orlando	4	0	0	0	0	2	1	.323
Cuthbert	4	1	2	1	0	1	0	.303
Hosmer	3	0	1	1	0	1	1	.278
Perez	0	0	0	0	1	1	0	.263
Escobar	3	0	0	0	0	0	2	.249
Butera	0	0	0	0	1	0	0	.282
Burns	0	1	0	0	0	2	1	.230
Mondesi	3	0	0	0	0	3	2	.204

Kansas City Royals Pitchers

	IP	H	R	ER	BB	SO	HR	ERA
Volquez (L)	6.0	10	4	4	1	2	0	5.04
Strahm	2.0	1	0	0	0	5	0	2.25
Soria	1.0	0	0	0	0	1	0	4.31
Herrera	1.0	3	3	3	0	1	1	2.13

GAME ACTION

Fans love to study the stats of their favorite players and teams. Players, managers, and **scouts** also pore over the numbers. Pitchers use stats to plan ways to attack batters. For instance, a pitcher might be more careful with a batter who has a long hitting streak. Some pitchers rack up a lot of strikeouts, while others get very few. Batters may change the way they swing the bat depending on the pitcher's statistics.

Managers use stats to decide where to position players on the field. With a power hitter at bat, the manager could have the fielders play farther back than usual. If a runner with many stolen bases reaches first base, the manager may move the players again. The infielders move closer to the bases to try to prevent a steal.

FANTASY AND THE FUTURE

Fantasy baseball is a game for adults that fans play by using the real statistics of MLB players. To play in a fantasy league, fans draft players to form teams. Fantasy teams are ranked based on the stats of the players. Most fantasy leagues allow team owners to add or drop players and to make trades with other owners. One study showed that nearly one in five adults in the United States plays fantasy sports.

With the popularity of stats among fans and those who play the game, the use of numbers in baseball will likely grow. MLB managers use stats in more interesting ways than ever before. In recent years, the infield shift has become popular. Using advanced stats, managers know where a batter is likely to hit the ball. They may shift their infielders to one side of the field, leaving the other side mostly empty. It will be fun to see where statistics take baseball next!

STATS MATCHUP

Mike Trout of the Los Angeles Angels and Bryce Harper of the Washington Nationals are two of baseball's biggest superstars. They began their MLB careers at about the same time. Fans love to compare the sluggers and argue about which player is the game's best.

Bryce Harper Washington Nationals	
2,336	At bats
651	Hits
412	Runs
122	Doubles
17	Triples
121	Home runs
334	Runs batted in
.279	Batting average
58	Stolen bases

BRYCE HARPER

Here are the statistics for their first five full MLB seasons (2012–2016). Who is MLB's best player? Trout has the advantage so far, but Harper is coming on strong.

Mike Trout
Los Angeles Angels

2,874	At bats
890	Hits
580	Runs
169	Doubles
37	Triples
163	Home runs
481	Runs batted in
.310	Batting average
139	Stolen bases

MIKE TROUT

GLOSSARY

earned run average (ERA): a statistic that stands for the number of runs a pitcher allows in a nine-inning game excluding scores from errors (unearned runs). To calculate ERA, divide the number of earned runs allowed by the number of innings pitched and then multiply by nine.

error: a mistake made by a fielder that allows a batter to reach base or a base runner to advance one or more bases

inside-the-park home runs: batted balls that don't go over the outfield fence but still allow batters to run all the way around the bases

no-hitters: complete games pitched by one pitcher in which no player on the other team gets a hit

on-base plus slugging (OPS): a stat that combines how often a batter reaches base with how often the batter gets an extra-base hit

save: a statistic for a relief pitcher who finishes a game by recording the last out with a lead of three runs or less

scouts: people who use stats and other information to judge the abilities of athletes

slugging percentage: total bases reached on hits divided by at bats. Slugging percentage gives a good idea of how many extra-base hits a player gets.

spitballs: pitches thrown with a ball that has saliva or sweat on it. Spitballs move in unusual ways and are hard to hit.

stolen bases: statistics given to base runners who advance by their own actions to a base they are not entitled to

Triple Crown: an award given to a player who leads the league in batting average, home runs, and runs batted in

FURTHER INFORMATION

Baseball Almanac
http://www.baseball-almanac.com

Baseball Reference
http://www.baseball-reference.com

Braun, Eric. *Super Baseball Infographics*. Minneapolis: Lerner Publications, 2015.

Jacobs, Greg. *The Everything Kids' Baseball Book: From Baseball's History to Today's Favorite Players—with Lots of Home Run Fun in Between*. Avon, MA: Adams Media, 2014.

Major League Baseball—Kids
http://mlb.com/kids

Reavy, Kevin, and Ryan Spaeder. *Incredible Baseball Stats: The Coolest, Strangest Stats and Facts in Baseball History*. New York: Sports Publishing, 2016.

Tejada, Justin. *Sports Illustrated Kids Stats! The Greatest Numbers in Sports*. New York: Time Home Entertainment, 2013.

INDEX

batting average, 7, 24, 28–29
box score, 24

comebacks, 21

Dead Ball Era, 4, 22

earned run average (ERA), 14, 24

fantasy baseball, 27

Hall of Fame, 23
hitting streak, 8–9, 26

home runs, 4–5, 11, 22–23, 24, 28–29

Live Ball Era, 5

saves, 17
Steroid Era, 5, 11, 22
stolen bases, 12, 26, 28–29
strikeouts, 16, 23, 24, 26

winning percentage, 18–19
wins, 13, 18

PHOTO ACKNOWLEDGMENTS

The images in this book are used with the permission of: © iStockphoto.com/Aksonov, p. 1; © iStockphoto.com/Aksonov (stadium background throughout); © Iconic Archive/Getty Images, p. 4; © iStockphoto.com/Steve Mcsweeny, p. 5 (top); © PETER NEWCOMB/AFP/Getty Images, p. 5 (bottom); © Vincent Laforet /Allsport/Getty Images, p. 6; © Justin K. Aller/Getty Images, p. 7; © Laura Westlund/Independent Picture Service, pp. 8, 11, 17, 19, 20, 23 (bar graph); © Elsa/Getty Images, p. 9; Tom Hauck/ Icon SMI 719/Newscom, pp. 10–11; © Focus on Sport/Getty Images, p. 12; AP Photo/Ric Tapia/Icon Sportswire, p. 14; © Rich Pilling/Major League Baseball/Getty Images, p. 15; AP Photo/Alex Brandon, p. 16; AFLO Sports/Newscom, p. 18; © JOHN G. MABANGLO/ AFP/Getty Images, p. 20; Brian Blanco/ZUMAPRESS/Newscom, p. 21; © The Sporting News/Getty Images, p. 22; Photography Collection, Miriam and Ira D. Wallach Division of Art, Prints and Photographs, The New York Public Library, Astor, Lenox and Tilden Foundations, p. 24; © Ed Zurga/Getty Images, p. 25; AP Photo/Dan Hamilton/Icon Sportswire, p. 26; © Blend Images/SuperStock, p. 27; © Jason Miller/Getty Images, p. 28; AP Photo/G. Newman Lowrance, p. 29.

Cover photos: © iStockphoto.com/Aksonov.